CONNEMARA

Vegetation and Land Use Since the Last Ice Age

MICHAEL O'CONNELL

Department of Botany, University College Galway

OPW

Oifig na nOibreacha Poiblí
The Office of Public Works

Dublin
1994

Text and photographs: Michael O'Connell
Drawings: Angela Gallagher
Design: *j*usty

© 1994 Government of Ireland

Government Publications Sale Office
    Sun Alliance House, Molesworth Street
        Dublin 2

ISBN: 0-7076-0412-5

Additional Illustrative material was made available by the following:
Justin King (Figs. 4.11 - 4.16)
Office of Public Works, Connemara National Park (Figs. 4.3, 4.5,4.8 and 4.17)
Department of the Environment, Northern Ireland (Fig. 6.6)
The maps reproduced in this publication are based on Ordnance Survey
Maps by permission of the Government (permit no. 5903)

CONTENTS

ACKNOWLEDGEMENTS

The account presented here would not have been possible without the research efforts of the following: Máire Bowler, Henk Heijnis, Chun Chang Huang, Eneda Jennings, Sinéad Keane, Rosemary McCormack, Karina McDonnell, Carol McMahon, Karen Molloy and Edel Ní Ghráinne. Through their endeavours in the Department of Botany, University College Galway, they have contributed substantially to the elucidation of various facets of the environmental history of Connemara. Míle bhuíochas díbh uile.

Thanks to Michael Gibbons for guidance with respect to the archaeological field monuments and for many useful discussions on the archaeology and history of Connemara.

Assistance with field work provided by Pádraic Cooke and Pat O'Rafferty, Department of Botany, University College, Galway, as well as by staff of the Connemara National Park, is gratefully acknowledged.

Special thanks to Noel Kirby, Park Superintendant, Connemara National Park, for the encouragement, help and advice received during preparation of this publication.

Financial assistance towards carrying out the research was received from the Office of Public Works (National Parks and Wildlife Service), ICI (Ireland) Ltd, and the Presidential Research Fund, University College, Galway.

FOREWORD

The interest of the Connemara landscape to the discriminating visitor will be greatly enhanced by reading this attractive handbook, written by Dr Michael O'Connell, and published by the Office of Public Works, which manages the Connemara National Park.

There could be no better author than Michael O'Connell who, from his base in University College Galway, has been carrying out important research work in this area for a long time. And it has not been carried out in isolation, because Michael has been in contact with workers in Europe, particularly Germany, for many years.

He gives an authoritative, but not over heavy, account of the natural history of the area, from the first appearance of a tundra flora when the Ice Age ended about 11 000 years ago. He traces the slow return of woodland, and shows that a visitor to the area 7000 years ago would have looked out on a canopy of rich oak woods, interspersed with stands of pine on poorer soils.

A visitor 3800 years ago would have heard the lowing of cows, and seen the first invading farmers beginning to clear away trees to create farmland. Through the following millennia, we witness the combined effects of human impact and climatic deterioration encourage the widespread development of all-embracing bog, and slowly the landscape we see before us takes shape. During the upsurge in population in the first half of the 19th century, reclamation of farmland expanded rapidly but, after the Famine collapse, the countryside slowly subsided into sleep. To-day the sleep becomes uneasy as intrusive patches of foreign conifers push into the landscape.

The story is unrolled before us in a judicious well-illustrated mixture of science and sympathy, and all visitors to the Park and the Connemara region will benefit from its study. The Office of Public Works and the author are to be congratulated on an attractive handbook.

Frank Mitchell
March, 1994

ILLUSTRATIONS

Explanation of Chapter time clocks

A pictoral representation of vegetation and cultural developments within a chronological framework is shown at the beginning of each chapter. A wheel with twelve spokes, each representing a millennium, is used. Age, in thousands of years, is indicated as years before present on the spokes of the wheel and as B.C./A.D. outside the rim of the wheel. Around the rim, cultural developments are indicated. The time slice(s) under consideration in a particular chapter is highlighted.

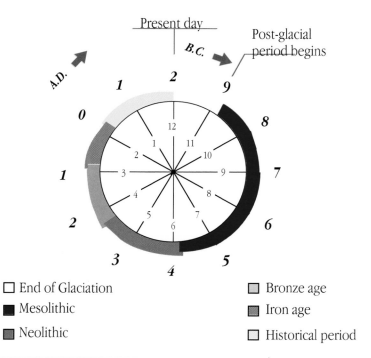

☐ End of Glaciation   ☐ Bronze age

■ Mesolithic   ■ Iron age

■ Neolithic   ☐ Historical period

Chapter No.	Vegetation/cultural developments	Time Periods	
4	Early shrub and woodland	9000 to 6000 B.C.	
5	Early (Neolithic) farming	6000 to 4000 B.C.	
6	Climax woodlands	4000 to 3500 B.C.	
7	Pine on bog Spread of blanket bog	2500 B.C. 1200 B.C.	
8	Woodland regeneration Woodland clearance	A.D. 0-300 A.D. 300-800	
9	Modern times	A.D. 1800 ➡	

• 1 •

Introduction

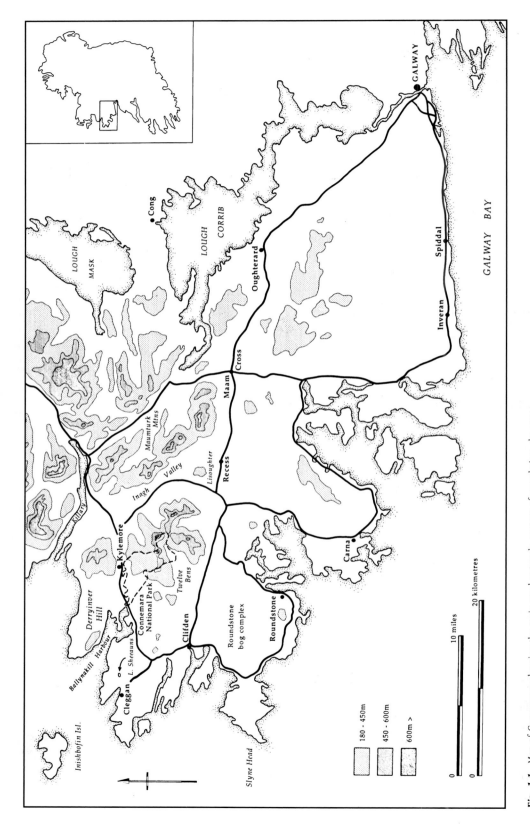

Fig. 1.1. Map of Connemara showing the main road network, centres of population, the area comprising the Connemara National Park, and the principal sites where scientific investigations into past land-use history have been made.

2

Connemara, according to the author and cartographer Tim Robinson, is 'the land that looks upon the Twelve Bens, that close knit, mandala-like mountain range, as its stubborn and reclusive heart'. Never having existed as an administrative unit, the boundaries of this region of great natural beauty and distinctive flora have never been officially defined. In this century, Connemara, or as preferred by some, Conamara, has come to denote that area of bog, lake, mountain and coast bounded by the shores of Lough Corrib on the east, the Atlantic Ocean on the west, and with Galway Bay and Killary Harbour forming its southern and northern boundaries, respectively (Figs. 1.1-1.3).

Unlike many Irish and indeed most European landscapes, where large prehistoric stone monuments and earthworks, medieval settlements and castles, and urban conurbations of varying size amply attest to a human presence over several millennia, the Connemara landscape is one where, to the casual observer at least, nature reigns supreme and the human presence does not unduly intrude. Yet, some 30 000 souls inhabit this region today, and, in the beginning of the last century, before the Great Famine took its toll, the population was, in some areas, up to ten times that of today. While the *bothán* or houses of the poor of the last century are now in ruins and have largely faded into the landscape, the patches of land once so assiduously cultivated are still clearly marked by ridges about a metre wide that invariably follow the slope of the ground to facilitate drainage. These ridges, best seen under

Fig. 1.2. View of the bog and lake-dominated landscape of the Roundstone peninsula. In these wetlands several of the plants for which Connemara is justly famous thrive. Especially noteworthy are the rare species of heather (e.g. Mackay's heath *(Erica mackaiana)*, the mediterranean heath *(Erica erigena)* and St. Dabeoc's heath *(Daboecia cantabrica)*) and also the American pipewort *(Eriocaulon aquaticum)*. It is also one of the main over-wintering stations in Ireland for the Greenland white-fronted goose *(Anser albifrons flavirostris)* and golden plover *(Pluvialis apricaria)*.

the light cast by the early morning or low evening sun, extend into the most inhospitable places (Figs 1.3 and 8.4). They remain as a stark reminder of those past times when a vast population, using human brawn and the spade, brought even the poorest soils under cultivation to produce the crop that gave the most bountiful return, namely the potato. Not surprisingly, the widespread failure of the potato in the years 1845 and 1846, resulted in a human disaster on a scale not experienced in Ireland since the Black Death in the fourteenth century.

In the pages that follow, the story that is sketched is not just that of the last few hundred years but extends back over several millennia. It is the story of how rocks, soils, climate, plant and animal life and last, but by no means least, the human presence have combined and interacted to give us what today we know as Connemara.

This account does not purport to cover all aspects of the events and processes involved in the shaping of the Connemara landscape. Indeed, the present state of knowledge is such that, in many respects, only the broadest outlines of the picture can be painted. However, it is hoped that the account will stimulate interest and help the local person and visitor alike to a greater appreciation of a region with great natural beauty.

Fig. 1.3. The intricate pattern of stone-walled fields near Inveran, S. Connemara. Now devoted exclusively to rough pasture these fields, carved out of peat-covered soils, once carried potatoes which were the main source of sustenance for a large population. Today, heathers and *Sphagnum* are slowly reclaiming their habitat once expropriated by human toil.

• 2 •

Sources of information

The story of the Connemara landscape as told in the following pages is pieced together from many sources. The written sources include travellers' accounts of excursions into Connemara, especially in the eighteenth and nineteenth centuries. There are also the important and detailed statistical data on farming and population (census data) that were collected systematically, firstly by the British Government beginning in 1847 and after 1921 by the Irish Government. For earlier times, however, the historical record is poor or indeed for much of the period non-existent, so that we have to rely on other sources of evidence. Firstly, there is the archaeological record that extends back to at least 7000 years ago. In this respect, we are fortunate in having at our disposal the results of the recently completed Archaeological Survey of County Galway. As a result of pains-taking survey by dedicated field workers over several years, our knowledge of the field monuments in the County has been greatly improved. This in turn provides important clues to human presence and activity not only in prehistory but also during the historical period.

A most important source of evidence for post-glacial environments is to be found in the form of fossils, and especially as pollen and other plant remains preserved in peat and in lake mud. The study of the fossil pollen record is referred to as pollen analysis and, since it forms the basis for the greater part of the reconstructions that follow, the technique is described in some detail (see box).

The fossil pollen record documents the natural vegetation, e.g. woodland, scrub, and bog,

How pollen analysis is carried out

1.   The initial step in a pollen analytical investigation is to sample peat or lake sediment by taking a vertical core from a bog or from the mud that has accumulated beneath the water in a lake basin. An ideal sampling site consists of a clean bank of turf left by peat cutters. From this, a long sod or monolith can easily be removed and brought to the laboratory for detailed sampling. In the case of a lake, various samplers are available that enable several metres of lake mud to be recovered, usually in one metre lengths, from beneath the lake water (Figs. 2.1 and 2.3).

2.   In the laboratory, sampling is carried out by removing small samples of peat or mud at regular intervals along the sod or core length (Fig. 2.3). The samples are sieved and chemically treated so that only the most resistant matter, namely pollen, remains.

3.   Using a microscope, the pollen is identified and counted (Fig. 2.4). The proportions of the different pollen types present in the samples are expressed as percentages of the total pollen counted in each sample (purely local pollen such as that from plants growing on the bog surface is excluded). The percentage results are then plotted in a pollen diagram (Fig. 4.4).

4.   The changes in pollen percentages from sample to sample, reflect changes in the composition of the past vegetation that were taking place as the peat or lake mud accumulated. The fossil pollen, therefore, provide us with a continuous record of plant life and, since plant life is greatly influenced by farming activity, we are also provided with, indirectly, a record of human activity in the landscape.

Fig. 2.1. Sampling a bog for pollen analysis. The sampler consists of several one-metre-long extension rods with a sampling chamber (normally a piston or pipe-like attachment) at the end. By adding extension rods one at a time, one metre thicknesses of sediment can be removed from successive depths. The photograph shows a sampler with extension rods left on, and with peat from depth 4-5 metres in the sampling chamber (see also Fig. 2.2).

Fig. 2.2. Peat, including wood of birch (*Betula*), recovered by the corer shown in the previous illustration. Each division on the scale lying beside the corer represents two centimetres.

particularly well. It can also provide important insights into human activity, and especially farming activity, through the presence of so-called human indicator pollen. The most important of these is ribwort plantain, *Plantago lanceolata* (Fig. 6.4), which normally indicates pastoral activity, and cereal pollen, which indicates that arable farming was being carried out in the vicinity of the sampling site.

Obviously, the attachment of a timescale to the various features recorded in a pollen diagram is of the utmost importance. Fortunately, all naturally occurring organic material has a built-in clock in the form of minute quantities of a radioactive isotope called carbon-14 (^{14}C). Measurement of the concentration of this isotope of carbon provides a radiocarbon-based chronology which is the basis for most of the age determinations used in the text (see also box).

For reconstructing glacial and pre-glacial environments, reliance must be placed on methods other than pollen analysis. Soft deposits, such as peats and lake sediments, cannot accumulate during a glaciation. Glaciations also normally destroy soft deposits formed during earlier warm periods or interglacials. Occasionally, interglacial peats and lake sediments do survive but, unfortunately, none have been discovered in Connemara to date. However, the geomorphologist and the geologist, by studying land forms and rocks, can tell us much about the glacial and pre-glacial history of Connemara. We will now turn our attention to some of these aspects since they have shaped the physical environment or stage on which our story unfolds.

Fig. 2.3. Part of a lake core having been sampled for pollen analysis. Slices of mud or sediment are removed for analysis at regular intervals, in this instance, every 4 cm. Occasional levels are marked so that the precise levels from which a particular pollen sample was taken can later be identified. This is especially important if samples are subsequently to be removed from particular levels for radiocarbon dating.

Fig. 2.4. Photograph of fossil pollen as seen under the microscope. The pollen, which are about 3000 years old, were preserved in the basal layers of blanket bog (core 3, Connemara National Park; see Fig. 7.5) to the south of the Connemara National Park Centre. The pollen are approximately 30 microns or 0.03 millimetres in diameter; to the naked eye they appear merely as dust.

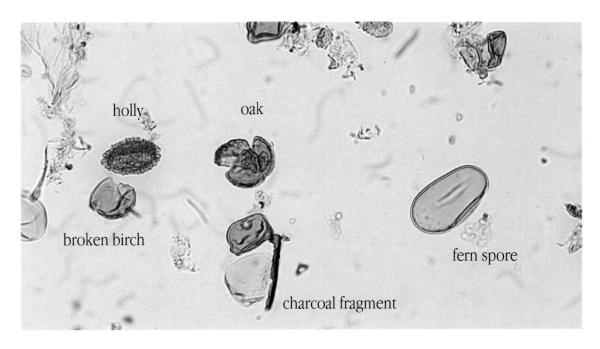

holly   oak

broken birch

charcoal fragment

fern spore

Chronologies and how they are established

Establishing the chronology or age of events for which there is no historical evidence was a major challenge to archaeologists and palaeoecologists prior to the discovery of radiocarbon dating in the early 1950's. Based on the fact that the concentration of the carbon-14 isotope (^{14}C) declines at a constant rate once an organism dies, the radiocarbon method enables us to estimate how long it is since organic matter, e.g. wood, charcoal, peat and bones, was part of a living organism.

A basic assumption of the method is that the concentration of ^{14}C atoms in the atmosphere has remained constant over thousands of years. In other words, it is assumed that the ratio of ^{14}C to ^{12}C (non-radioactive and stable) atoms at the time the organism was alive was similar to that pertaining in more recent times. We now know that this basic assumption is, in fact, false so we must calibrate or adjust the dates provided by the radiocarbon laboratory so that they are equivalent to calendar years.

Calibration of radiocarbon dates has been made possible as a result of an international radiocarbon calibration programme of recent years in which Queen's University, Belfast has played the leading role. Calibration has involved radiocarbon dating, to a high level of precision, wood samples of known age. Most of the wood used has come from Irish oak timbers recovered from old buildings, archaeological sites and, in the case of the older samples, from oak trunks recovered from various bogs in Northern Ireland. The age of the wood is determined by dendrochronology, i.e. the study of the pattern of annual tree-ring widths. The age obtained by the radiocarbon method is then compared with that provided by dendrochronology. This enables a correction factor to be established for each radiocarbon date.

Through the international radiocarbon calibration programme, correction factors are now available for the period extending back to the end of the last glaciation. Using these correction factors, radiocarbon results from any time within this interval can be corrected or calibrated.

The dates cited in this text are calibrated dates, i.e. the radiocarbon determinations of age have been corrected so that they correspond to calendar or 'real' years.

•3•

Beginnings

Connemara is an ancient land. Indeed, the region has its beginning near the start of geological time, over 600 million years ago. Most of the rocks that form the central and north-western part of Connemara were initially laid down in a relatively shallow sea at a time when eastern Canada and much of north-west Europe were part of the one landmass. Later, as a result of a complex series of earth movements and metamorphosis, these rocks have been altered in various ways to form, on the one hand, the relatively soft schists of the valley floors and lowlying lands of Central Connemara and, on the other hand, the extremely hard and erosion-resistant quartzites that constitute the Beanna Beola, or Twelve Bens, and the Maumturk Mountains. At about 400 million years ago, there was a large intrusion of igneous rock, i.e. granite, in the southern part of the region. These granite rocks, together with the more ancient volcanic rocks of the Roundstone area, are the foundation of the greater part of the area that stretches from Slyne Head to the western outskirts of Galway City.

The more spectacular scenery of the region owes much to processes dating to the most recent geological period, namely the Quaternary or, as it is commonly called, the Great Ice Ages. Connemara was severely glaciated during the last two glacial periods. The landscape has, therefore, been substantially affected by glaciation and, as might be expected, it is the most recent Ice Age that has had the greatest impact. At the height of the last glaciation, about 23 000 years ago, glaciers covered most of north-west Europe from Scandinavia to Connemara and as far south as the mouth of the

Fig. 3.1. Oak-dominated woodland on an island in Lough Inagh. In the background are the Twelve Bens. Ice movement during the last glaciation deepened the valley floor and left bowl-like depressions or *cirques* high up in the mountain sides. Regeneration of woodland (foreground on island) has taken place this century as a result of a reduction in grazing pressure.

Shannon and beyond into Co. Limerick. Most of Connemara lay under a thick cover of ice, with only the higher mountain peaks protruding through the ice sheet. On these exposed peaks, referred to as nunataks, a severe, cold and harsh environment prevailed comparable to the severest of arctic conditions today. So, little or no life existed in this pristine, more or less completely snow and ice-covered landscape.

As the great ice sheets or glaciers moved from the uplands into the low-lying lands, they created many of the more spectacular features of our present-day landscape. The glaciers sculptured the mountains by removing great volumes of rock and leaving behind bowl-like depressions on the mountain sides known as *cirques* or *corries*. After the ice melt, these cirques frequently retained water and formed mountain lakes or tarns. In the lowlands, large U-shaped valleys were formed by the moving glaciers. The U-shaped Inagh valley, flanked on both sides by mountains moulded smooth by ice and with large and spectacular corries, is a splendid example of glacial activity (Fig. 3.1).

Elsewhere in Connemara, one sees the results of deposition of the crushed rock from the ice sheets. To the west of Kylemore Abbey, a river of melting water within the ice, i.e. an *esker* (from the Irish *eiscir*, i.e. gravel ridge), deposited sands and gravels that are at present being quarried for road making and as building material. In the Cois Fharraige area of southern Connemara, deposition was minimal and often in the form of isolated drumlins (see front cover) or large granite boulders which were later to be covered by blanket bog.

These ice-transported boulders, referred to as erratics, are particularly conspicuous in the area about Spiddal. In general, the ice sheets in Connemara, unlike those in Central Ireland, deposited little drift (sand, silt clay and boulders) with the result that, over large parts, there is little suitable parent material available to form fertile soils. This, and the subsequent soil deterioration or podzolisation and growth of blanket bog, have resulted in, at best, marginal land in terms of modern day farming over much of Connemara.

The last glaciation ended rapidly. For reasons that are not yet fully understood, the ice sheets began to retreat and a fast melt set in, so that shortly before 14 000 years ago, conditions were such that plant life could re-establish itself. However, a severe down-turn in climate occurred at about 12 000 years ago. This is referred to as the Younger Dryas cold phase because of the large quantities of *Dryas* (mountain avens) leaves that are sometimes found in lake sediments laid down during this time. Conditions were such that ice sheets formed again in the mountains and, even in the lowlands, the climate was too severe for most animal life. During this time, the Giant Irish Deer became extinct in Ireland. The climatic down-turn, however, was of relatively short duration, especially when one considers the magnitude of the oscillations involved. By approximately 11 000 years ago, or 9000 B.C., temperatures had again risen, the snow had melted, and the re-colonization of Ireland by plants, animals, and soon also by people, commenced. We will now trace the history of recolonization and the subsequent shaping of the Connemara landscape.

• 4 •

Greening of the landscape and the first woodlands (9000 to 6000 B.C.)

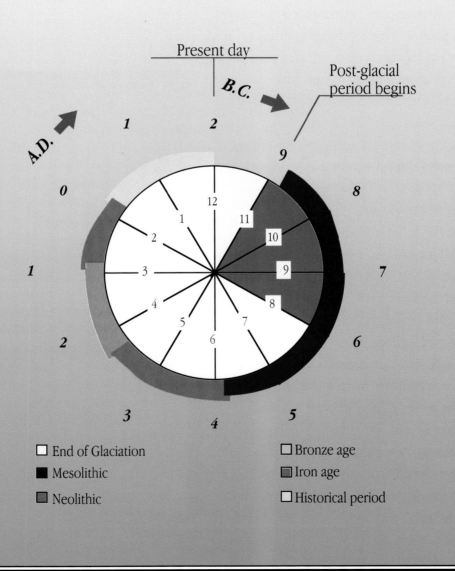

Present day

B.C.

Post-glacial period begins

A.D.

□ End of Glaciation
■ Mesolithic
▨ Neolithic

□ Bronze age
▨ Iron age
□ Historical period

As the last Great Ice Age came to an end somewhat more than 11 000 years ago, a new land surface was available for colonization by plants and animals. These spread into Ireland mainly from southern and central Europe and, presumably, via Great Britain. At this time, the seas had not yet risen to their present level and so land bridges or land connections existed between Ireland and Britain and also between south-eastern England and continental Europe.

The first land plants were mainly herbs and low shrubs such as grasses, sedges, various dock *(Rumex* and *Oxyria)* species, and also low shrubs. These early colonisers had to cope with what must have been rather adverse conditions with respect to both climate and soils. The climate, while it warmed up quickly, showed a considerable degree of continentality and the soils were as yet unstable due to frost action and they were also low in key nutrients such as nitrogen.

Like the Arctic and Alpine floras of today, the early post-glacial floras were colourful and varied. Plant groups that were well represented included the pink family, e.g. various species of catchfly *(Silene and Lychnis* species), and the stonecrop *(Sedum)* and saxifrage *(Saxifraga)* families (Figs. 4.1 and 4.2). Many of the species present then have a rather restricted distribution in Ireland today (e.g. mountain avens, *Dryas octopetala*) and, indeed, others are absent altogether (e.g. dwarf birch, *Betula nana*). Some species, such as the purple saxifrage *(Saxifraga oppositifolia),* probably survived through the final cold phase at the end of the last Ice Age. Today, it is found in the uplands of Connemara, but at Lisoughter it has been recorded at the exceptionally low elevation of 135m.

Fig. 4.1 The purple saxifrage, *Saxifraga oppositifolia*, photographed in the French Alps at 2700 m in its typical habitat of bare soil where a snow patch has just melted.

Fig. 4.2 The yellow mountain saxifrage, *Saxifraga aizoides*. It usually grows where soil conditions are unstable. In the early post glacial, the unstable conditions would have resulted mainly from severe frost action. Its particularly colourful flowers, must have resulted in spectacular displays during late spring and summer.

Fig. 4.3 One of the first shrubby species to become established was the dwarf willow *(Salix herbacea)*. Like all willows, this species is dioecious, i.e. there are separate male and female plants. The photograph is of a male plant with pollen-producing flowers. The dwarf willow survives in the mountains of Connemara to this day.

With the spread of plant life and a decrease in the duration and frequency of frost, inwash of soil into lakes and other basins ceased, the soil surface stabilised, and the organic and nitrogen content, and overall fertility of the soil improved. This, together with improvements in climate, facilitated the establishment of more warmth-demanding species including the meadowsweet *(Filipendula ulmaria)* and various shrubs.

The first shrubby vegetation almost certainly included the dwarf willow *(Salix herbacea,* Fig. 4.3) which tolerates harsh conditions especially if it is protected from the severity of winter conditions by snowbeds. This shrub was quickly followed by crowberry *(Empetrum nigrum)* and juniper *(Juniperus communis,* Figs. 4.4 and 4.5). Both of these plants are found mainly in upland areas of Connemara today, juniper sparingly and invariably in its creeping or prostrate form while the crowberry continues to be an important constituent of upland heath and mountain bog. At about 8000 B.C., these two species played a rather different role. They dominated much of the landscape and probably achieved optimum development in sheltered areas in the lowlands. At the same time, the numerous lakes that were scattered over the lowlands supported a rich flora that included water-milfoils *(Myriophyllum)*, pondweeds *(Potamogeton species)*, white water lilies *(Nymphaea alba)*, water mint *(Mentha aquatica)* and water crowfoots *(Ranunculus)*.

With continuing improvement in climate and soil conditions, new species began to colonise the landscape. Tree willows such as *Salix cinerea* arrived, but it was not until the arrival of silver birch *(Betula pubescens)* that the landscape took

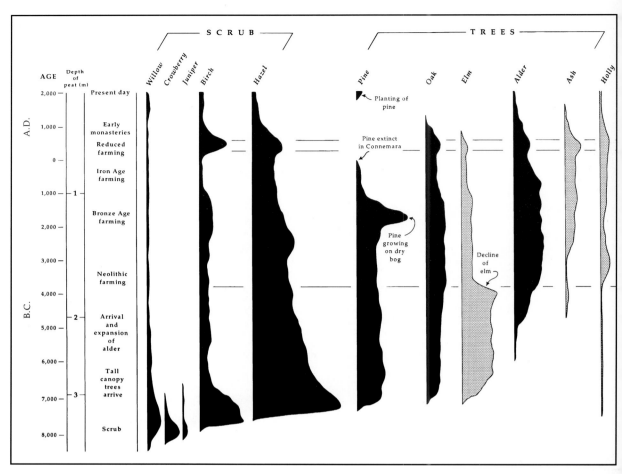

Fig. 4.4. Simplified pollen diagram (core 1) from the Connemara National Park. This records the vegetation development on the bog surface (see the pollen curves for the bog plants on the right hand side of the diagram) and the surrounding landscape. The record begins at about 9000 B.C. (base of diagram) and extends to recent centuries (the uppermost layer of the bog has been damaged due to peat cutting; hence a record for the last few centuries is not available at this site).

Fig. 4.5. With increase in temperatures, juniper (*Juniperus communis*) scrub came to dominate large areas of Connemara. Like willow, juniper is also dioecious. Specimens bearing pollen producing cones (male plant) and the typical blue-black berries (female plant), respectively, are shown.

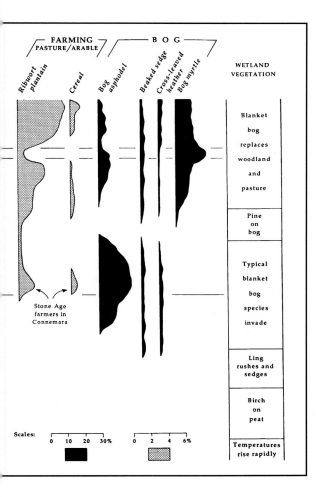

on a radically new appearance. Silver birch invaded the juniper scrub and the crowberry-dominated heathlands, and soon birch woodlands comparable to those found today in the northern boreal regions were widespread (Fig. 4.4).

The birch-dominated vegetation, however, in turn succumbed to hazel *(Corylus avellana,* Fig. *4.6)* which, under present day conditions, plays the role of a pioneer woodland species. Hazel is more intolerant of cold conditions than birch so its arrival suggests a further improvement in climate. The pollen record indicates that thickets of hazel, similar to those we see today in the Burren, Co. Clare, quickly covered the landscape. Open areas were now confined to the exposed coastline and lake margins. Here, herbaceous plants such as the plantains *(Plantago* species*)*, the cow-wheat *(Melampyrum pratense)* and the royal fern *(Osmunda regalis,* Fig. 4.10) continued to survive. The mountain tops probably still supported the heath communities that had been established several hundred years before.

Tall canopy trees did not invade until about 7700 B.C. (Fig. 4.4). The first to do so was the Scots pine *(Pinus sylvestris,* Figs. 4.7 and 4.8), which, in the context of Britain and Ireland, has survived without interruption to the present day only in Scotland. This tree, which could cope with poor soil conditions such as provided by the granite rocks of southern Connemara, soon became dominant over large areas. Where better soils prevailed, as in much of north-west Connemara, oak *(Quercus)* became the main tall canopy tree. While we cannot tell from the pollen which oak species was involved, we may assume that it was the Irish or sessile oak *(Quercus petraea,* Fig. 4.9), i.e. the main canopy-forming species of our present day western oak woodlands.

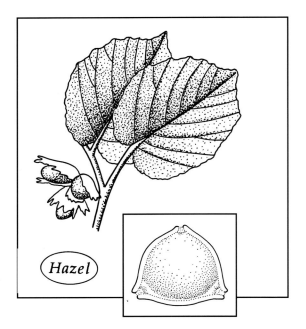

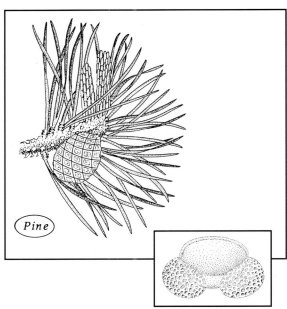

Fig. 4.6. The hazel *(Corylus avellana)* assumed the role of dominant woody species shortly after 8000 B.C. and continued to be of importance for at least the next 4000 years. Its nuts were an important food source for prehistoric peoples. The inset shows the pollen of hazel, a characteristically smooth grain with three pores. Note: in this and the drawings of plants that follow, the pollen is in each case magnified approximately 1000 times with respect to the leaves.

Fig. 4.7. Pine *(Pinus)* produces vast quantities of pollen which, with its two air bladders (see inset), is well adapted for dispersal. It is regarded as being over-represented in the pollen record, i.e. its contribution to the vegetation cover is normally less than its percentage pollen representation in the fossil record would suggest.

Fig. 4.8. Male cones of Scots pine *(Pinus sylvestris)* with clouds of freshly released pollen.

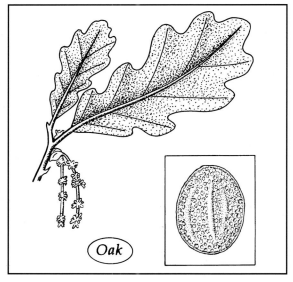

Fig. 4.9. The oak (drawing shows the Irish oak, *Quercus petraea*), with drooping catkins in which its the characteristic, rather rough-walled, pollen with three slits (inset) are produced.

20

Elm (*Ulmus*, Fig. 6.7), which was so important on the fertile soils of central Ireland at about this time and later, never played a significant role in these western woodlands. Its main competitor, oak, was probably favoured by the generally lower soil fertility.

Rowan or mountain ash (*Sorbus aucuparia*) flourished under natural openings in the canopy where mature trees were knocked by storm or simply died from natural causes. We may also assume that broad-leaved whitebeams such as the Irish whitebeam *(Sorbus hibernica)* and *Sorbus aria* were also present.

With the increasing diversity of plant life, there was a corresponding development in the fauna. Large animals would have included brown bear *(Ursus arctos,* Fig. 4.11), wolf *(Canis lupus,* Fig. 4.12)* and wild boar *(Sus scrofa,* Fig. 4.13)*. As regards the smaller animals, fox *(Vulpes vulpes)*, pine marten *(Martes martes,* Fig 4.14), stoat *(Mustela erminea,* Fig. 4.15)*, otter *(Lutra lutra,* Fig. 4.16)* and Irish hare *(Lepus timidus)* were all probably present.

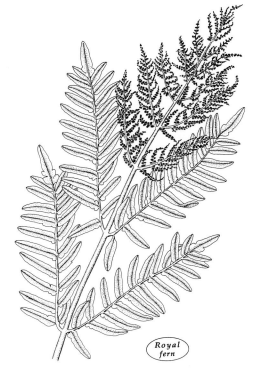

Royal fern

Fig. 4.10. The royal fern, *Osmunda regalis,* is certainly regal in stature. In favourable locations it grows to about 3 m in height. An unusual feature is the manner in which the upper part of the leaf or frond is modified to produce the reproductive structures which, as in all ferns, consist of spores. Today, this fern is common throughout western Ireland but is relatively rare elsewhere in the country.

Fig. 4.11. The brown bear *(Ursus arctos)*, remains of which are known from as early as the Mesolithic period, may have survived in Ireland until the early Christian period (A.D. 400).

21

Fig. 4.12. The wolf *(Canis lupus)*, which survived in Ireland until near the end of the eighteenth century, depended on large mammals such as deer as a food source. The threat it posed to cattle and sheep, rather than to humans, led ultimately to its extinction which occurred considerably later in Ireland than in Britain.

Fig. 4.13. The wild boar *(Sus scrofa)* was probably once common in Connemara. Finds of wild boar remains in Ireland are mainly from the early Mesolithic, i.e. the early post-glacial. The wild boar is an excellent swimmer and so, while its spread would have been facilitated by the existence of landbridges, these are not essential in explaining its early presence.

Fig. 4.14. The pine marten *(Martes martes)*, a species mainly of woodland but also to be found in open habitats such as the Burren, has been recorded in recent times from coniferous plantations in eastern and central Connemara. Its earliest records in Ireland are from early Christian contexts but it should be borne in mind that its small bones may have gone unnoticed in archaeological excavations (same applies to the stoat) which are the main source of fossil animal bone.

Fig. 4.15. The earliest records for the stoat *(Mustela erminea)* in Ireland come from early Christian contexts. It should be noted that there is no evidence that the weasel *(Mustela nivalis)* ever existed in Ireland, though stoats are often referred to in rural areas as weasels.

Surprisingly, bones of red deer *(Cervus elaphus)* dating to this early period have not been recorded in Ireland. Red deer was, however, present prior to the arrival of the first farming cultures or *Neolithic* peoples (see Chapter 6). In the skies, the white tailed and golden eagles *(Haliaëtus albicilla* and *Aquila chrysaetos,* Fig. 4.17*)* were probably a common sight.

Fig. 4.16. The otter *(Lutra lutra)* was once widely hunted for its fur and also because of its perceived threat to fishing. It is still common in Ireland where it is protected by law. Remains of the otter have not been recorded from earlier than Bronze Age contexts.

Fig. 4.17. The white-tailed *(Haliaëtus albicilla)*and golden eagle *(Aquila chrysaetos;* shown here) nested in Connemara until well into the last century.

• 5 •

Primeval woodlands
(6000 to 4000 B.C.)

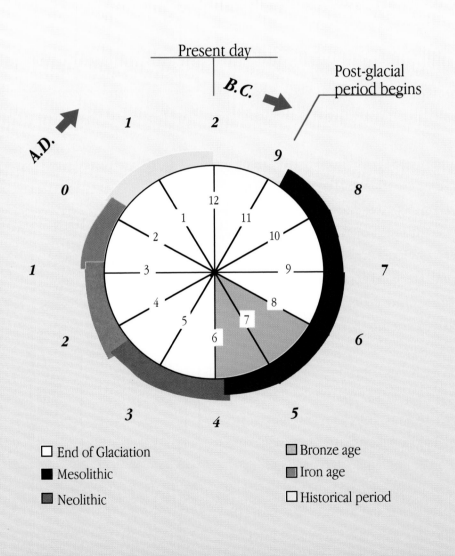

Present day

B.C. ➤

A.D.

Post-glacial
period begins

□ End of Glaciation   ▨ Bronze age

■ Mesolithic   ▨ Iron age

▨ Neolithic   □ Historical period

At the beginning of this period, woodlands dominated the Connemara landscape from coast to coast and also to a considerable height on the mountain sides. Lakes were more numerous than today as many water bodies existed that later developed reedswamp. With the passage of time, the reedswamp was overgrown by bog and so in this way many lakes disappeared, as it were, from the landscape. In the wet valleys where carr, i.e. birch and willow-dominated vegetation growing on peat, flourished considerable depths of peat had already accumulated (Fig. 4.4). This peat consisted mainly of the partially decomposed remains of birch, sedges, grasses, rushes *(Juncus)* and ling *(Calluna)*. The phenomenon that is now referred to as blanket bog did not yet exist.

At about 6000 B.C. another tree assumed importance for the first time. This is the alder *(Alnus glutinosa,* Fig. 5.1), a species of wet habitats. The date for the expansion of alder varies considerably from place to place. In the Connemara National Park, for instance, it did not expand until about 5000 B.C., while elsewhere in Connemara it was abundant at least 800 years earlier.

Why expansion of the alder population was delayed in the National Park area we do not know. A similar erratic pattern of expansion of alder is know from other regions in Ireland and indeed from north-west Europe generally. The expansion of alder is regarded by pollen analysts as marking the beginning of the *Atlantic* period when the climate was probably wetter and warmer than today. How far the spread of alder was influenced by climate change is uncertain. It is more likely that a series of

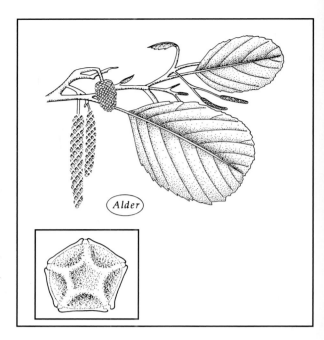

Fig. 5.1 The alder *(Alnus glutinosa)* is common today in wet habitats such as lake and stream margins, and wet hollows. Its seedlings are known to be sensitive to spring frosts which may have been a factor militating against its expansion in the early post-glacial.

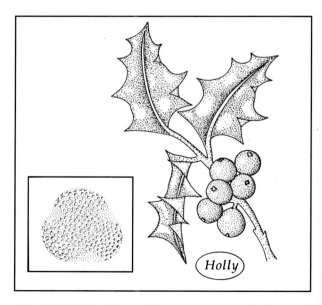

Fig. 5.2 The holly *(Ilex aquifolium)*, is an evergreen shrub or small tree that is sensitive to winter frosts. It grows particularly well in the present-day mild oceanic climate of western Ireland. The pollen record indicates that, from at least 4500 B.C., it was an important component of the oakwoods in western Ireland. Increased human disturbance of the tall canopy woodland, which resulted in increased light reaching the shrub and ground layers, probably favoured holly.

chance events, such as small scale disturbance in the primeval woodlands, rather than any overall increase in rainfall determined the spread of this tree.

The mature deciduous oakwoods of this period were undoubtedly species-rich. In the canopy layer some elm was present and, where soil conditions were particularly poor, pine would have competed successfully with oak. Birch, rowan and especially hazel were important in the shrub layer. Holly (*Ilex aquifolium*, Fig. 5.2) too was important, and ivy *(Hedera)* and honeysuckle *(Lonicera periclymenum)* were also present. There was a rich ground flora consisting of a variety of ferns including bracken *(Pteridium)*, polypody *(Polypodium)*, and filmy and buckler ferns *(Hymenophyllum*, Fig. 5.3, and *Dryopteris* species). We may assume that mosses and liverworts were also abundant though we lack fossil evidence. Most of these plants do not produce readily identifiable spores nor are the plants themselves readily preserved in peat or lake sediment.

In contrast to the oak woodlands, the pine forests may have been more open and bore little resemblance to the dense blocks of trees in commercial forests of today. Ling *(Calluna)*, grasses and bracken fern *(Pteridium)* were important elements of the ground flora in these woodlands. Here also the capercaillie *(Tetrao urogallus*, Fig. 5.4), a bird that survived in Ireland down to the end of the eighteenth century, flourished.

At this time there is evidence that soils were becoming progressively more acidic and hence less

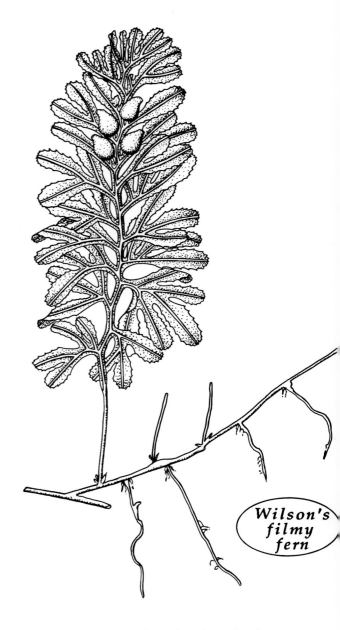

Wilson's filmy fern

Fig. 5.3 Recent research has shown that Wilson's filmy fern *(Hymenophyllum wilsonii)* was common in the oak woodlands of Connemara. The Tunbridge filmy fern *(Hymenophyllum tunbrigense)* as well as the Killarney fern *(Trichomanes speciosum)* were probably also present though, to-date, fossil evidence to support this is not available.

Fig. 5.4. The capercaillie *(Tetrao urogallus)*, a bird associated with coniferous woodlands, probably flourished in the ancient pinewoods of Connemara.

Fig. 5.5. Red grouse *(Lapogus lapogus)*, once common, is now a rare sight in Connemara due to a decline in heather cover as a result of burning and over-grazing.

fertile. The tall canopy woodlands, however, persist though hazel has declined in importance. In depressions within valleys, peaty areas including birch carr are now being invaded by *Sphagnum* moss. This had the effect of acidifying the local mire or wetland and drastically altering habitat conditions so that a whole new suite of plants could invade. Bog species such as bog asphodel *(Narthecium ossifragum,* Fig. 5.6) and beaked sedge *(Rhynchospora)* as well as several *Sphagnum* species could now flourish in the valley mires (Fig. 4.4). However, several millennia were to elapse before these species initiated widespread blanket bog formation. The red grouse *(Lagopus lagopus,* Fig. 5.5) populations were probably favoured by increased availability of suitable food sources such as ling *(Calluna).*

It is also during the Atlantic period, that we find the first evidence in our pollen records for the American pipewort *(Eriocaulon aquaticum,* Fig. 5.7), which may well be regarded as the hallmark of the present-day lake flora of Connemara where it has its north-west European headquarters. Its pollen is first recorded in the mid Atlantic period, i.e. at about 5000 B.C. To date, its distinctive pollen has been consistently recorded only in a few cores, mainly from the Carna and Roundstone areas and also from Inishbofin. The infrequency of the fossil records suggests that, in the past, this species was not as widespread in Connemara as today.

The earlier history of the American pipewort is somewhat of an enigma. Did it survive the Ice Ages (it has also been recorded from interglacial deposits in Ireland which indicates that it was present during

Fig. 5.6 The yellow-flowered bog asphodel *(Narthecium ossifragum)*, is common today in the wetter parts of the blanket bogs of Connemara. The pollen record shows that it has been an important component of the wetland flora of the Connemara National Park for at least 7000 years.

29

an earlier warm period dating to approx. 200 000 years ago) or did it migrate from some refugium that existed in the warmer south as the glaciers melted and temperatures rose? Satisfactory answers to these questions we may never have. On the other hand, the long post-glacial history of the species in Connemara leads us to rule out introduction by human agency.

No mention has been made of the role of people in this early post-glacial environment. To date, the only archaeological evidence for a human presence in these early times comes from the Oughterard area of north-eastern Connemara. Here, the flints and scrapers of Mesolithic peoples who lived by hunting, fishing and gathering wild berries and hazel nuts, have been found. These peoples, who were entirely dependent on and lived in tune with nature, had relatively little impact on their environment and, moreover, probably avoided dense woodland. Future research will, undoubtedly, find traces of Mesolithic activity elsewhere in Connemara.

Fig. 5.7. Photograph of American pipewort *(Eriocaulon aquaticum)* growing in shallow lake water in Connemara.

First farmers
(4000 to 3500 B.C.)

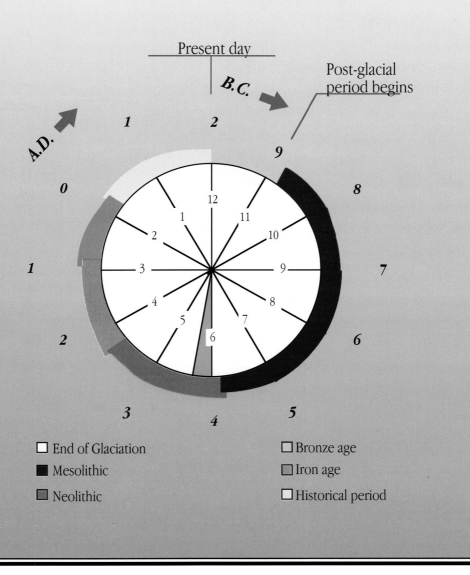

At about 4000 B.C. a series of changes was initiated in the Connemara landscape that had profound consequences. A new element was introduced into the biological environment which, up to now, was largely in equilibrium with itself and with the physical environment of soil and climate. Neolithic peoples arrived or, at least, Neolithic culture spread into the region. Neolithic, which literally means New Stone Age, is the archaeological term used to describe the first farming cultures. These peoples, who relied solely on stone implements, introduced to the region cereal growing (most likely wheat and barley) and brought with them domesticated animals that included cattle, sheep and goats.

The after-life must also have been of great importance to the Neolithic peoples, since they expended considerable energy in the construction of megalithic tombs (Fig. 6.1). In Connemara, these graves, known also as Giant's Graves or *Leaba Dhiarmuid agus Ghráinne* (bed of Diarmuid and Gráinne from the epic legends of the Fianna) are to be found almost exclusively in a triangular area, the apices of which are defined by Clifden, Cleggan and Kylemore. Within this area, more than 30 megalithic tombs have been recorded. They provide striking evidence for a substantial Neolithic population, at least in this part of Connemara. The archaeological record is complemented by the pollen evidence from lake muds and peats which enables us reconstruct how these early farmers impinged on the environment and the type of farming they pursued.

We are fortunate in having a particularly good record of the activities of these early farmers in the pollen preserved in the lake mud at Lough Sheeauns, east of Cleggan (Fig 6.2). The presence of several megalithic tombs in the vicinity of the lake led to the selection of this lake as a source of sediment for detailed pollen analytical investigations, the result of which will now be considered.

Fig. 6.1. Megalithic tomb, wedge type, on the Atlantic coast at Salerna, west of Cleggan.

Fig. 6.2. Aerial view of Lough Sheeauns, near Cleggan. The road to Cleggan appears in the lower part of the photograph. Beside the road is a portal dolmen (PD), with capstone displaced during road widening. To the south of the lake is a court tomb (CT) datable to the early Neolithic and also a stone alignment (SA) which may date to the Neolithic or Bronze Age. A core was taken from the centre of the lake for the purpose of carrying out pollen analytical investigations.

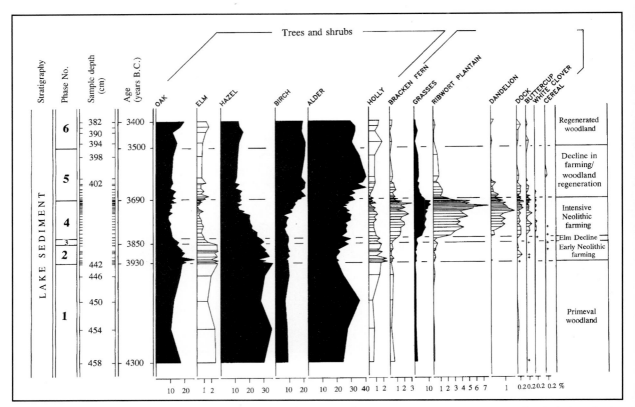

Fig. 6.3. Part of a pollen diagram from L. Sheeauns showing the changes in pollen percentage representation associated with the introduction and expansion of farming at the beginning of the Neolithic. Between 402 and 442 cm (depths are indicated with respect to the top of the sediment), inclusive there is continuous sampling, i.e. every centimetre of sediment has been analysed, which gives a continuous record; elsewhere sampling is at 4 cm intervals. Pollen curves with low values have been exaggerated and are not shaded; '+' is used to indicate the occasional presence of a pollen type (less than 0.001% of the pollen counted in the particular sample). Note that the vertical axis is based on time (years) rather than depth.

Fig. 6.4. Grassland dominated by ribwort plantain (*Plantago lanceolata*) in Errislannan, south-west of Clifden. The early Neolithic pastures probably appeared quite similar to this.

The pollen evidence for Neolithic farming and the impact of the first farmers on the primeval woodlands at Lough Sheeauns

One of the most immediate tasks facing the first Neolithic people was to create openings in the dense primeval woodlands to enable them to carry out farming, especially arable farming. On the basis of the pollen record from L. Sheeauns (Fig. 6.3), the nature and extent of the clearances and time scale involved can be reconstructed in considerable detail. The sequence of events is as follows:

1. The primeval woodland composition consisted mainly of oak, hazel, alder and holly, and small amounts of pine, elm and birch (phase 1, Fig. 6.3).
2. The first generation or two of farmers that settled in this far western part of Ireland appear to have made little impact on the natural environment. In the pollen record relating to this time (phases 2 and 3, Fig. 6.3), holly *(Ilex)*, and ribwort plantain *(Plantago lanceolata)* are consistently present in moderate quantities for the first time. On the other hand, the amount of pollen of oak and hazel reaching the lake sediment remains steady or even increases.

The increase in holly and ribwort plantain suggests that small clearances were made in the dense tall canopy woodland which enabled plants associated with open spaces to flower freely. Though the overall tree population was now smaller, tree pollen production actually increased. This was in response to greater availability of light due to the newly created small scale openings.

In the pollen record, the first cereal pollen are noted.

Fig. 6.5. Emmer *(Triticum dicoccum)*. This early species of wheat had its origins in the Near East almost 10 000 years ago and was introduced into Ireland in the early Neolithic, about 4000 years later.

These were produced by wheat and represent the earliest evidence from Connemara of cereal cultivation. Interestingly, these records are as early as those available from any other part of Ireland. Which species of wheat was sown we cannot say from the pollen but evidence from elsewhere in Ireland, consisting of charred remains of cereals found in the course of archaeological excavations, suggests that it was most likely emmer *(Triticum dicoccum*, Fig. 6.5).

We can expect that these early farmers also had domesticated animals (Fig. 6.6). The oak-dominated woods would have provided copious supplies of acorns for pigs in autumn. For cattle, open spaces as such were not required; these would have grazed in the now relatively open woodlands which also provided shelter in winter. We have no evidence that these peoples constructed byres for their cattle. Byres were hardly required because the winters at that time were milder than at present.

3.   This low level of farming soon changed to a particularly intensive phase during which there was a much greater impact on the natural environment. In the pollen record, the tree pollen falls by twenty percentage points, grass pollen increases and the pollen of ribwort plantain rises from less than 1% to almost 8% of total pollen (phase 4, Fig. 6.3). These changes signify more of less total clearance of the oak-dominated woodland in the vicinity of the lake. The woodland was replaced by pasture, evidence for which comes not only from the increased representation of the pollen of grasses and ribwort plantain (see Fig. 6.4) but

Fig. 6.6. A pictorial reconstruction of life in the Neolithic. For the first time, life was essentially sedentary. Woodlands were cleared so that cereals could be cultivated and pastures created for grazing by cattle and sheep, while pigs were fattened on the acorn masts.

also from the substantial amounts of dandelion-type (*Crepis* and *Taraxacum* species), buttercup (*Ranunculus*) and chickweed (*Cerastium*) pollen. Surprisingly, there is little evidence of arable farming. Only the occasional cereal pollen is recorded during this time. Then, as now, the emphasis appears to have been on pastoral farming. This intensive phase of early Neolithic activity lasted only about 150 years, i.e. about 5 or 6 generations. It was followed by a period of equal length during which woodlands regenerated as a consequence, presumably, of declining population and farming activity (phase 5, Fig. 6.3). Evidence from other areas suggests that, at this time, many other parts of Ireland experienced a similar decline in agricultural activity.

We assume that the megalithic tombs in the vicinity of L. Sheeauns were constructed during the intensive phase of activity, i.e. almost 6000 years ago or almost a millennium before the main phase of pyramid construction in Egypt. Where the Neolithic culture spread from we do not know but it almost certainly arrived by a sea route, which was much more easily negotiable than overland. Neolithic tools were limited to stone axes which could be readily fashioned from local stone. Though extremely primitive in present-day terms, these were effective implements in cutting down the dense woodlands. Fire, which was certainly known and used by these peoples, appears not to have been employed in the clearance of woodlands around L. Sheeauns. The amount of charcoal particles recorded in the lake sediment was minimal and does not support the supposition that fire was used to any significant extent at this site.

It is also worth noting that, unlike Céide Fields in north Mayo, where the Neolithic populations laid out over 1000 hectares (2500 acres) of field systems with stone wall boundaries, no evidence for such early field systems have been found to date in Connemara. It is intriguing to think that the early farming communities in the neighbouring counties of Galway and Mayo, both of whom built similar type tombs, appear to have managed that most valuable resource, the land, in a very different way.

Causes of the Elm Decline at 3850 B.C. — the evidence from Lough Sheeauns

The so-called Elm Decline, i.e. a rather dramatic decline in elm pollen representation at 3850 B.C., is one of the most spectacular features in pollen diagrams from north-west Europe. It is also to be seen in most Irish pollen diagrams including those from Connemara, even though here the elm pollen representation is never high (Fig. 6.3; also Fig. 4.4).

What caused such a profound change over a wide geographical region has long been debated by pollen analysts. Various explanations have been put forward including:

1. climate change — this would readily account for a synchronous change over a wide area. How climate change could have adversely affected elm, and elm alone, cannot however be readily explained.

2. human impact — the decline in the elm pollen curve in most pollen diagrams coincides with the first records for cereal and ribwort plantain (*Plantago lanceolata*), i.e. the spread of Neolithic or farming cultures. How stone-age farmers could have brought about such a fundamental change in the vegetation cover of an area as extensive as north-west Europe within a century or so is difficult to comprehend.

3. disease — the recent widespread destruction of elm trees caused by the Dutch Elm Disease, indicates the potential of disease to effect rapid and widescale change in an elm tree population. Unfortunately, fungal spores do not fossilise well and so the chances of finding direct proof, in the form of fungal spores, for the presence of a fungal

Fig. 6.7. Elm *(Ulmus)* produces a pollen (see inset) with a worm-like pattern on the outer surface of its wall and with pores (normally five or more) lying on one circumference. The differences in the pollen produced by the various species of elm are so small as to make it extremely difficult to assign fossil pollen to a particular species.

38

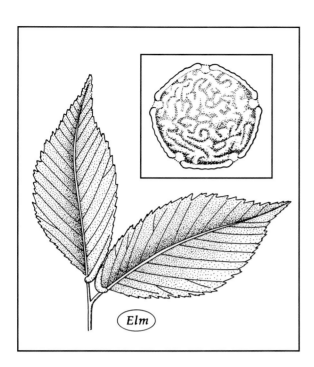

Elm

pathogen such as *Ceratocystis ulmi,* the cause of Dutch Elm disease, is very small indeed.

The pollen diagram from L. Sheeauns (Fig. 6.3) is important in that it provides an exceptionally detailed record of the various changes that took place in the period before, during and after the Elm Decline and, furthermore, a series of radiocarbon dates provides a secure chronology for the events recorded at this site. In considering the causes of the Elm Decline, the following features in the pollen diagram are considered to be of some significance:

• In the century prior to the Elm Decline, Neolithic farming commenced (see Phase 2, Fig. 6.3 and note the presence of wheat and ribwort plantain pollen) but large-scale woodland clearance did not take place. This clearly shows that the spread of Neolithic farming cultures takes place *before* the Elm Decline and allows us to eliminate the possibility of a direct link between the arrival of Neolithic farming and the Elm Decline (see 2, above).

• At the Elm Decline, the elm pollen representation is more than halved but other tree pollen curves are largely unchanged (Phase 3, Fig. 6.3). In other words, elm alone appears to be affected. Also, it is interesting that it is not until Phase 4 that the pollen indicators of farming show increased representation, which again suggests that there may be no direct connection between farming activity and the Elm Decline.

The most plausible explanation for the

events, as recorded at L. Sheeauns and also several other sites, is that the rapid decline in the representation of elm is mainly the result of a disease that affected elm trees only. There is no direct evidence for the nature of the disease but we may envisage that it was similar to that commonly referred to as Dutch Elm disease. This epidemic is caused by the fungus, *Ceratocystis ulmi*, which is spread from tree to tree by the beetle *Scolytus scolytus*. If this beetle were present (this is not as far fetched as it may seem; its fossil remains have been recorded from pre-Neolithic contexts in Hampstead Heath, London), the small openings in the dense woodlands made by the earliest farmers would have greatly favoured flight by the beetle, which prefers open spaces. So human activity, while not directly involved, may have at least facilitated the rapid spread of disease and so may be indirectly linked with the Elm Decline at 3850 B.C.

• 7 •

Changes in the natural environment in the late Neolithic and later Bronze Age (2500 to 1200 B.C.)

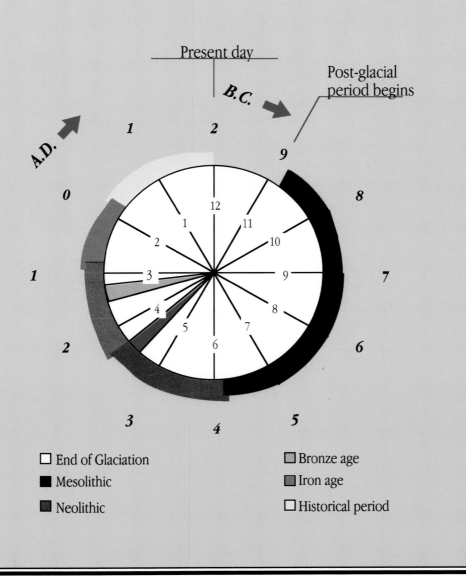

Present day

B.C.

Post-glacial period begins

A.D.

☐ End of Glaciation
■ Mesolithic
■ Neolithic

☐ Bronze age
■ Iron age
☐ Historical period

All the evidence available to date suggests that the early Neolithic, i.e. the period of the early Stone Age farmers, was a time of great diversity in the Connemara landscape. We can envisage small settlements of several families living at the edge of or in areas more or less totally cleared of trees. In these clearances, herbs associated with pasture as well as plants of disturbed ground, including arable land, could expand for the first time since the end of the Ice Age. In the valleys, bog vegetation flourished but had not yet spread out to envelop potentially good farming land, and numerous lakes dotted the landscape, some of which would later be infilled by the partially decomposed remains of reedswamp and bog vegetation. Apart from these open areas of natural and human origin, primeval woodlands covered the lowlands.

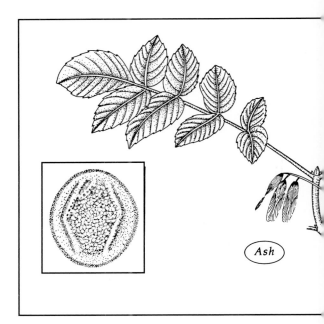

Ash

For reasons we do not understand, the first Neolithic populations declined after an initial spurt of woodland clearance and farming, so that evidence of human activity almost disappears from the pollen record at L. Sheeauns for almost 700 years (Fig. 6.3, phase 6; the complete record is not shown). Nature had now a chance to reassert itself and woodlands recovered. The balance which previously existed was, however, now disturbed and so new combinations of trees and other plants were possible. We will trace some of these developments, beginning with changes that took place in the centuries about 2500 B.C.

Changes in woodland composition at about 2500 B.C.

After a disturbance, nature seldom reverts to precisely the same point that it was at prior to disturbance. Our long pollen records from Connemara illustrate this very well. In the formerly cleared areas about L. Sheeauns, birch at least

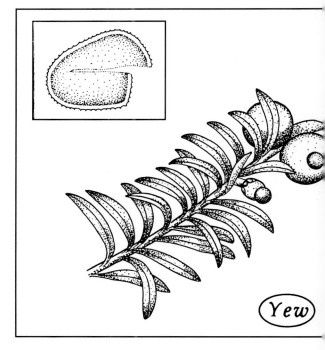

Yew

Fig. 7.1. Ash *(Fraxinus)*, while present from probably at least 6000 B.C., only expanded during woodland regeneration following early Neolithic clearances. Its pollen (see inset) has a fine reticulate or net-like pattern on its wall and has three slits (one behind the plane of the drawing and therefore not shown).

Fig. 7.2. Yew *(Taxus)*, like ash, took advantage of the openings created in the primeval woodlands by the early Neolithic farmers. Its pollen (see inset) has a rather unusual shape and has only one slit which make it rather distinctive; yet it has often been overlooked by pollen analysts.

partially displaced hazel *(Corylus)* as the main undershrub in the regenerated woodlands (Fig. 6.3, top of diagram). Elm *(Ulmus)*, which was never important, played a still more minor role. Its place may have been partly taken by ash *(Fraxinus*, Fig. 7.1), the pollen of which now consistently appears for the first time (Fig. 4.4; a slender pollen curve for ash has been omitted from Fig. 6.3).

In the Spiddal area of southern Connemara, more dramatic changes are recorded. In the regenerated woodlands, ash and especially yew *(Taxus*, Fig. 7.2) expanded and the latter, together with oak *(Quercus)*, became the main canopy tree for a short time. We assume that both the yew and ash expanded into the clearances left by the Early Stone Age farmers as their numbers diminished. Pine was also present in the Spiddal area, but compared with the early primeval woodlands it now had a much diminished role (see also below).

The expansion of yew, with its dark evergreen and potentially poisonous foliage, must have greatly altered the woodlands and the overall appearance of the landscape. The rich ground flora associated with oak woodlands could not survive in the dense all-year-round shade cast by the yew, the dead foliage of which also poses a threat to cattle. In Connemara, as in the rest of Ireland, yew is rare today. Rather surprisingly, it is relatively common in woodlands on lake islands in Connemara, regeneration having been facilitated by the reduction in grazing pressure from cattle and sheep during this century.

The phenomenon of pine forests growing on bogs (2500 B.C.)

As already mentioned above, pine had already declined in importance as farming was first introduced to Connemara. It was, however, to flourish once more but this time not as a tree of normal woodland. Rather, it succeeded in establishing itself on bog surfaces (Figs. 7.3 and 7.4). In western Ireland today pine or oak trees are seldom, if ever, seen growing on bogs, the surfaces of which are much too wet for trees. Bogs carry plantations, mainly of lodgepole pine *(Pinus contorta)* and spruce *(Picea)*, which succeed in becoming established mainly because drainage is carried out prior to planting. At some point in the past, however, bog surfaces must have become sufficiently dry to enable trees to become established on them without any artificial drainage having been carried out.

In the Connemara National Park, we see particularly good evidence of a natural pine forest on bog in the form of pine stumps exposed by peat cutters before the area became part of the National Park (near location of core 1, Figs. 7.5 and 7.6). In peat from the same level as the stumps, there is an abundance of pine pollen, indicating that these pine trees flowered well and produced much pollen (Fig. 4.4).

This pine forest succeeded because the bog surface dried out sufficiently to allow pine seed to germinate, establish seedlings and grow to mature trees. Detailed microscopic examination of the peat from levels about the pine stump layers give us a good impression of the ground layer of these woodlands. The previously present bog asphodel *(Narthecium ossifragum)* and sedges *(Carex species)*, which require a wet bog surface, were replaced mainly by ling *(Calluna)* and also cross-leaved heather *(Erica tetralix)*.

Pine stumps can be seen at or near the base of most bogs in Connemara. This has given rise to the popular conception of blanket bog spreading out, enveloping the woodland and killing it. This, however, may not be correct. Rather it appears that

Fig. 7.3. A pine stump near Spiddal, south Connemara, part excavated by peat cutters. The stumps are resting on several centimetres of peat which insulated the tree from the mineral ground, its more usual rooting medium.

Fig. 7.4. A pine stump in the Connemara National Park showing a large side root that may have been produced as a response to an increasingly wetter bog surface. A peat sampler is included for scale; its chamber, the bottom of which rests on the bog surface, is one metre long.

pine invaded where peat had already begun to accumulate. In the Connemara National Park, over two metres of peat underlie the pine stumps at the point where the peat was sampled for the purpose of constructing the main pollen diagram (core 1, Figs. 7.5 and 7.6). Pine stumps resting directly on the mineral ground, as might be expected if the bog spread to envelope existing woodlands, are seldom encountered (Figs. 7.3 and 7.4).

The important question as to what caused the bog surface to dry out should also be considered. Was it connected with a stage in bog development or was there a period of decreased rainfall and/or higher temperatures that caused the normally wet surface to become drier? A clue is provided by the evidence from several sites in western Connemara which shows that, at approximately 4500 B.C., woodland on bog was a widespread phenomenon. This suggests that there is some factor, operating at a regional level, that resulted in dry bog surfaces. This is most likely climate and, specifically, a shift towards drier and/or warmer conditions.

We may envisage a period with lower precipitation and/or higher temperatures at about 4500 B.C. that facilitated the establishment of pine on peat. Once the pine forest was established, it would have absorbed considerable quantities of water for transpiration and so contributed to lower water table levels in the bog. Todate, there is little evidence to suggest that seed produced by pine growing on bogs in western Connemara succeeded in establishing a number of generations of bog pine trees. The postulated dry period was probably not of sufficiently long duration to allow this to take place.

It might also be noted that another popular belief that *gius* or bog deal consists largely of oak does not square with the facts where Connemara is concerned. Oak stumps do occur in the

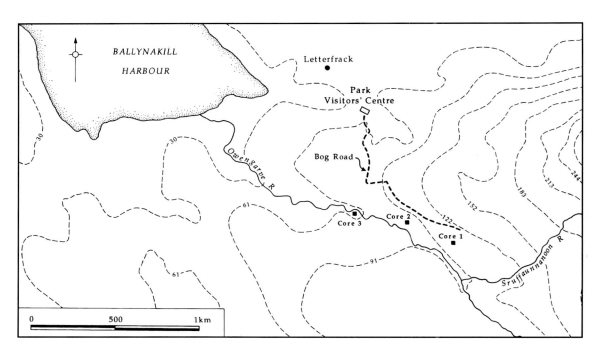

46

Fig. 7.5. Map showing the locations where sampling for pollen analysis was carried out in the Connemara National Park. Core 1: main pollen profile (material sampled: peat only); cores 2 and 3, short profiles (material sampled: blanket bog peat and underlying mineral soil). The main contours, in metres, are also shown.

Fig. 7.6. Aerial view of approximately the same area as shown in Fig. 7.5 with position of sites sampled for pollen analysis indicated. Diamond Hill is outside the photograph to the bottom right hand side.

Connemara bogs but are rare. The vast majority are pine and, very occasionally, timbers of yew are encountered.

The spread of blanket bog at about 1200B.C.

As has been described above, bog vegetation was established at valley sites long before the arrival of the first farmers in the early Neolithic. The spread of blanket bog, however, is a phenomenon that post-dates the advent of these peoples. An obvious pointer to this is the discovery over the years by peat cutters of megalithic tombs within blanket bog with the stones of the tombs resting, not on peat, but on mineral soil. The spread of bog must therefore have begun *after* the erection of these megaliths. So, the question remains: when and in what circumstances did the spread of blanket bog take place? Investigations within the Connemara National Park and on nearby Derryinver Hill have provided much new evidence bearing on this question.

Within the Connemara National Park, investigations have centred on two sites to the south of the Centre where blanket bog covers gently sloping ground to the north of the valley bog (locations 2 and 3, Fig. 7.5). At both these locations, samples were taken from the peat and the mineral soil beneath (Fig. 7.7). The pollen in the mineral soil provides evidence of the vegetation that existed for some time, probably centuries, prior to the growth of peat. That in the immediately overlying peat reflects the local and regional vegetation as the bog began to grow (Fig. 7.8).

At both locations, the pollen record shows that woodland existed in the centuries prior to bog growth. This woodland was dominated by oak in

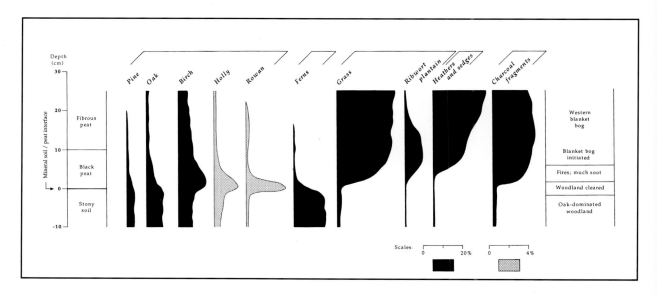

Fig. 7.7. Photograph of a pit face showing the basal peat and underlying mineral soil at sampling location 2, Connemara National Park (see Fig. 7.5). Sampling was carried out here for pollen analysis. Note the dark basal peat (tip of spade). Microscopic investigations showed that the dark colour arises from fine charcoal particles, the product of frequent firing of the vegetation at or near the sampling site. The light brown uppermost peat has been disturbed by peat cutting in the recent past; this has made it unsuitable for pollen analysis.

Fig. 7.8. A simplified pollen diagram based on pollen analytical investigations of mineral soil and overlying peat at locations 2 and 3, Connemara National Park (see Fig. 7.5). This provides a record of the changes in soil, vegetation and land use at about the time peat began to grow.

which grew Wilson's filmy fern *(Hymenophyllum wilsonii,* Fig. 5.3) and presumably also a rich carpet of mosses and liverworts similar to that occurring in present day western oak woodlands. Then, at 1300 B.C. according to the radiocarbon dates, this natural woodland was at least partially cleared. Holly *(Ilex)* and rowan *(Sorbus aucuparia)* expanded in the openings created in the woodland. Mor humus or acidic organic matter accumulated on the mineral soil. In this humus, the seeds of rushes *(Juncus)* are preserved and charcoal dust or soot is abundant. The presence of rush seeds indicates that the soil was wet, while the soot particles must be the product of repeated burning of the vegetation. By filling the soil pore space, which constitutes approximately 25% of a well-drained soil, the soot contributed to increased soil wetness by impeding the downward movement of water. The greatly increased soil moisture content favoured the initiation of blanket bog.

As we move higher up in the peat, the colour is jet black as a result of an abundance of microscopic charcoal particles (Fig. 7.7). The pollen from these levels indicate that bog species such as ling, sedges, *Sphagnum* and bog asphodel *(Narthecium)* have invaded; in other words, a plant community similar to present day blanket bog communities has become established. Within a century or two, it appears that woodland was replaced, firstly, by a heathy grassland that later gave way to bog.

As can be seen from the above, there appears to be a close connection in the Connemara National Park between fire and the development of blanket bog. Burning produced a fine soot that, not only slowed down drainage, but also prevented growth of woody species which absorb considerable quantities of water from the soil.

What caused the fires is difficult to ascertain with certainty. It is possible that they were natural,

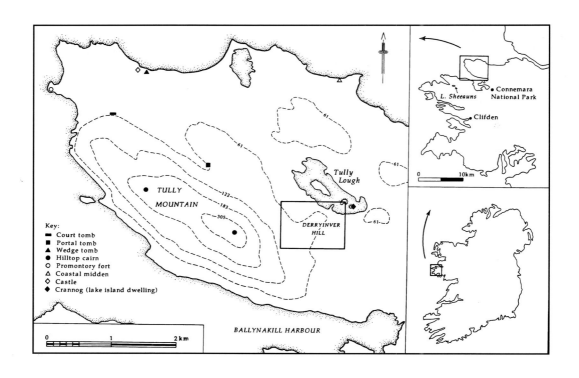

Key:
- ■ Court tomb
- ■ Portal tomb
- ▲ Wedge tomb
- ● Hilltop cairn
- ○ Promontory fort
- △ Coastal midden
- ◇ Castle
- ◆ Crannog (lake island dwelling)

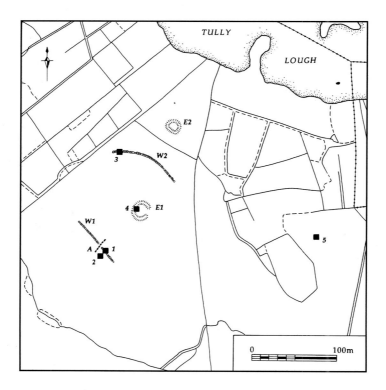

Fig. 7.9. Map of the Renvyle peninsula showing the location of the main archaeological field monuments (for features on Derryinver Hill, i.e. the area delimited by a box, see Fig. 7.10). Contours are shown in metres.

Fig. 7.10. Map showing the location of the main features on Derryinver Hill. These include the six-stoned alignment (A), pre-bog walls (W1 and W2), and two enclosures (E1 and E2) both of which are almost completely covered by peat. Pollen diagrams are available for locations 1-5 as follows (age of the top of the mineral soil/base of the peat is given in brackets):

1. mineral soil beneath stone wall near the alignment (500 B.C.)
2. mineral soil and overlying peat to south of wall near the alignment (A.D. 200)
3. mineral soil beneath curved stone wall (500 B.C.)
4. peat from ditch inside enclosure, E1 (1200 B.C.)
5. a 5 m long profile from the peat at the base of the Hill (9000 B.C.)

e.g. caused by lightning. However, it is more likely that these fires were deliberately caused by human agency. At about this time or a century or two later in other parts of north-western Connemara, a distinct upsurge in human activity is recorded in the pollen record. This suggests a substantial increase in population and farming activity datable to the later Bronze Age. We can assume that, with the knowledge of metal-working, the potential for human impact on the natural environment increased substantially. Part of that impact appears to be a regular firing of vegetation which, in the short term, would have stimulated grass production, but, in the longer term, had catastrophic effects on the local environment.

While we see the main phase of blanket bog development in Connemara occurring during the Bronze Age, i.e. from about 2500 to 1000 B.C., it would be incorrect to think that it was confined to this period. On nearby Derryinver Hill, on which stands a fine alignment consisting of six large upright standing stones, the discerning visitor will see a stone wall protruding through the thin cover of bog (Figs. 7.9-7.12). The wall runs over the hill at right angles to the alignment. The stones of this wall rest not on the bog but on the mineral soil beneath, showing that it was laid out prior to bog growth (Fig. 7.12).

Radiocarbon dates have shown that the pre-bog wall at the alignment and also the curved wall some distance to the north (Fig. 7.10) were constructed at about 500 B.C., i.e. in the mid Iron Age. The base of the peat, at some distance from the wall (location 2, Fig. 7.10) has also been radiocarbon dated. The dates obtained suggests that peat initiation began as late as A.D. 250.

The pollen record indicates that, from the time the stone wall was laid out in the mid Iron Age to

Fig. 7.11. View of the stone alignment on Derryinver Hill. A stone wall, more or less completely hidden by a thin covering of peat, intersects the alignment (W1 in Fig. 7.10; see also Fig. 7.12). The laying out of the wall probably considerably post dates the construction of the stone alignment which may have taken place in the late Neolithic or Bronze Age.

peat initiation at the end of the Iron Age, i.e. several hundred years later, the hillside was used not only as a pasturage but also that some cereals were grown. Then, at the end of the Iron Age, there was a distinct decline in farming activity not only here but also elsewhere in Connemara (Fig. 4.4). During this time, Derryinver Hill was no longer farmed, ling and grasses (presumably purple moor grass, *Molinia*, and mat grass, *Nardus*) took over, *Sphagnum* invaded and bog developed. This sequence of events, which involved the overgrowing of marginal agricultural land by bog, is being repeated today in several parts of Connemara. Fields that only a few decades ago carried potatoes are now developing a thin covering of peat as a result of changes in land use and farming practices (see Fig. 8.4).

Fig. 7.12. Part of the stone wall (W1 in Fig. 7.10) that intersects the stone alignment on Derryinver Hill. The thin covering of peat has been removed preparatory to sampling the mineral soil beneath the stones of the wall for pollen analysis. The stones rest on mineral soil rather than peat which shows that the local environment was quite different when the wall was laid out by Iron Age farmers at about 500 B.C.

•8•

End of the primeval forests and
early Christian settlements (A.D. 0 to 800)

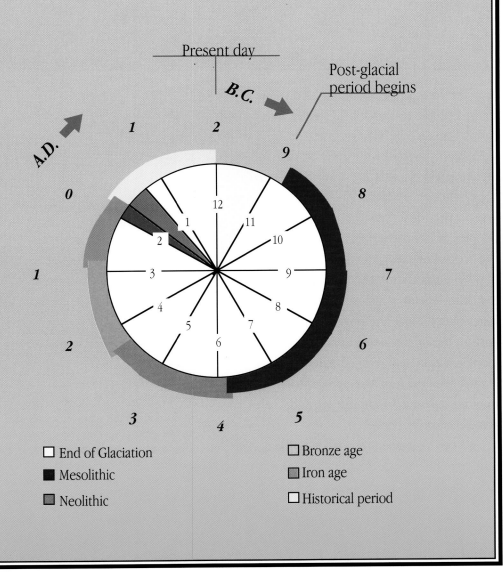

The Iron Age is regarded as the Age of the Celts, a people that once held sway in Europe from the Balkans to the Atlantic coast. In Ireland, the Celts are associated with cattle rearing and cattle stealing. This is well illustrated by *An Táin Bó Cuailnge* or the Cattle Raid of Cooley, an epic legend that describes the conflict between the peoples of Connacht under Queen Méabh against the peoples of Ulster over the red bull of Cooley.

We do not know the precise period in which the *Táin* legend, which goes back to prehistoric times, is set. Since the pollen records from many parts of Ireland, including Connemara, suggest that farming activity had reached particularly low levels at the end of the Iron Age (approx. A.D. 100-400), it may be assumed that the legends refer to a somewhat earlier period.

Woody vegetation responded to the decline in farming and staged a comeback in most parts of Connemara including the Connemara National Park (see phase marked 'Reduced farming' in Fig. 4.4). Birch and hazel regenerated to form extensive scrub and even oak woodlands were re-established

Fig. 8.1. Middens, i.e. sand dunes which, in the past, were colonised by peoples who lived mainly off shell fish and left their waste, namely, empty shells, bones, etc., on the dunes. This waste material is the hallmark of the midden. The photograph shows extensive middens, south of Clifden. The habitation layers, which were stable surfaces at the time of occupation, appear brown due to higher organic content. The covering sand is, at present, being whipped away by the winter gales, exposing these former occupation layers and leading eventually to their destruction and the inevitable loss of important evidence of past peoples and their environment.

in areas that were farmland for centuries. Pine, however, did not respond to the decline in human activity; it was now extinct and, furthermore, its habitats on the poorer soils were now covered by bog, the surface of which was too wet to carry trees.

The early centuries of Christianity, on the other hand, saw an upsurge in agricultural activity in most parts of Ireland, and Connemara was no exception (Fig. 4.4). Much of the remaining tracts of woodland, which now consisted almost entirely of oak, were cleared. Elm, never very important, may have become almost extinct. Open landscape supporting pasture and, where soil fertility permitted, arable farming, replaced scrub and woodland. The drier parts of the lowland blanket bogs and also the upland bogs and heaths were probably, as is the case today, used as an additional source of grazing.

The coastal parts of western Connemara appear to have been an important focus of activity in the early Christian period (Figs. 8.1 and 8.2), and, on the islands off the western coast, several monastic settlements were founded during this time. Among the more important was the monastery founded in A.D. 665 by St. Colman beside Church Lough on Inishbofin, off Cleggan (Fig. 8.3 and 8.4). The historical records suggest that this was a particularly important foundation in the early Irish Church. It was also a seat of learning, and tradition recorded that it attracted hundreds of students who came from other parts of Ireland and probably also from abroad (St. Colman, himself, returned from Iona, western Scotland, to establish this monastery). It was of sufficient importance that, in the Annals of the Four Masters written in the seventeenth century, the names of the abbots from the foundation of the monastery down to

Fig. 8.2. Detail of a midden where the wind has stripped away much of the overlying sand leaving strewn on the exposed surface mainly limpet shells *(Patella vulgata)*, the occasional oyster shell *(Ostrea edulis)* and teeth of cattle. The artifacts that have come to light in these sites and also the radiocarbon evidence, indicate that these midden sites were occupied mainly in the early Christian period.

A.D. 918 are listed. The present ruined church at the site probably dates to the thirteenth century (Fig. 8.3).

Recent pollen analytical investigations of the lake mud from Church Lough have confirmed the picture provided by the historical records. At a depth in the mud that corresponds to the time of the founding of the monastery by St. Colman, there is a dramatic change in the pollen content of the core. The representation of birch and hazel pollen declines and, instead, large quantities of grass, plantain and above all cereal, mainly wheat, pollen are recorded. To date, this is the only site in Connemara which has provided evidence of a farming economy where cereal production played such an important role. We can envisage a monastic settlement that, in this sheltered eastern part of the island, produced enough wheat for its own needs. Indeed, it was probably completely self sufficient as regards food. Timber, however, must have been in scarce supply and was probably imported from the mainland. Settlements such as these were not, however, as isolated as it may appear. The sea served as a highway and, no doubt, facilitated regular contact with communities on nearby islands and on the coastal fringes of mainland Connemara.

Fig. 8.3. Ruins of the medieval church to the east of Church Lough, Inishbofin, where once stood St. Colman's early Christian monastery.

Fig. 8.4. Church Lough, Inishbofin with abandoned cultivation ridges in the background. The ridges were most likely used for growing potatoes and were probably abandoned some time in this century. The white objects floating in the lake mark the positions where coring of the lake sediment was carried out for pollen analysis.

•9•
Final stages in the evolution of the present-day Connemara landscape (from A.D. 1800)

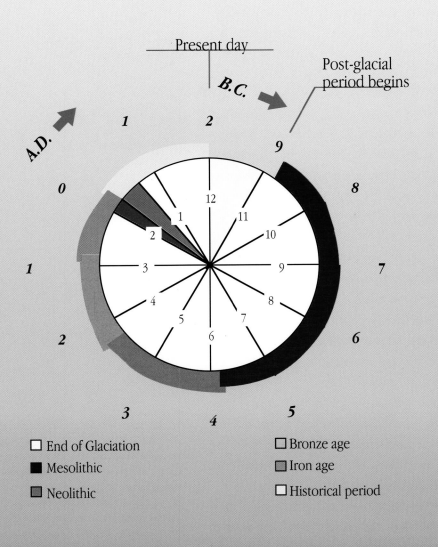

☐ End of Glaciation   ☐ Bronze age

■ Mesolithic   ◼ Iron age

◼ Neolithic   ☐ Historical period

Travellers' accounts of Connemara from the seventeenth and eighteenth centuries tell of a bog-covered landscape, bare of trees and extremely difficult of access due to the lack of bridges and roads. Then, beginning in the nineteenth century, a gradual transformation took place. At this time, the town of Clifden was founded by John D'Arcy, while in the latter half of the century (1864-1870), the neo-Gothic house, known today as Kylemore Abbey, was built by the wealthy Manchester merchant and philanthropist, Mitchell Henry (Fig. 9.1). The century saw the opening up of the region through the construction of a communication network consisting of roads and, at the end of the century (1893), the Galway to Clifden railway was completed.

As elsewhere in Ireland, the region has experienced major demographic and social changes in the last 200 years (Fig. 9.2). In the early part of the last century population expanded, land holdings were divided and there was increasing, and what subsequently proved to be fatal, dependence on the potato as a source of food. The failure of the potato crop due to blight, especially in the years 1845 and 1846, resulted in a sharp population decline though death and emigration (Fig. 9.2).

The decline in population continued throughout the latter part of the nineteenth century and, at the same time, there was a shift from arable to pastoral farming (Figs. 9.2 and 9.3). The Land Acts provided the mechanism for transfer of land from landlord to tenant. This also had a fundamental effect on the landscape, in that it provided the trigger for the construction of stone wall boundaries or so-called striping of the land.

By the beginning of the twentieth century most of the elements of the present landscape were in place. Tenants had acquired ownership of the land

Fig. 9.1. Aerial view of the Kylemore area with the Abbey at the lake edge and the neo-Gothic church nestling in the oak-dominated woodlands. The first Ordnance Survey maps, which date to 1839, show only low scrub. Woodland regeneration has been facilitated by control of grazing by cattle and sheep. Sadly, the woodland understorey is dominated by rhododendron *(Rhododendron ponticum)*. This introduced shrub, while having attractive flowers, destroys the rich fern and moss flora normally associated with such Atlantic oak woodlands.

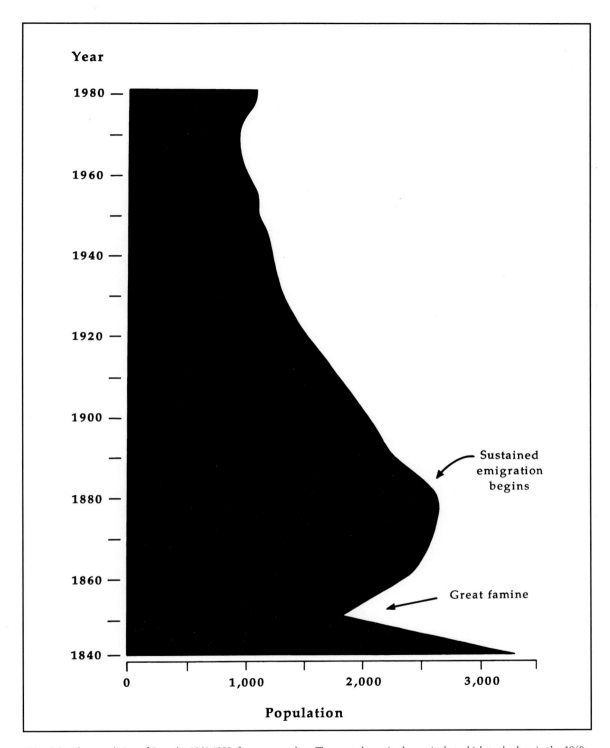

Fig. 9.2. The population of Renvyle, 1841-1980, from census data. The most dramatic change is that which took place in the 1840s when the population was almost halved as a result of the Great Famine. From the 1880's onwards, the decline reflects emigration rather than death from hunger and disease. The first reversal in the downward trend appears in the 1970's when a small rise in population was recorded.

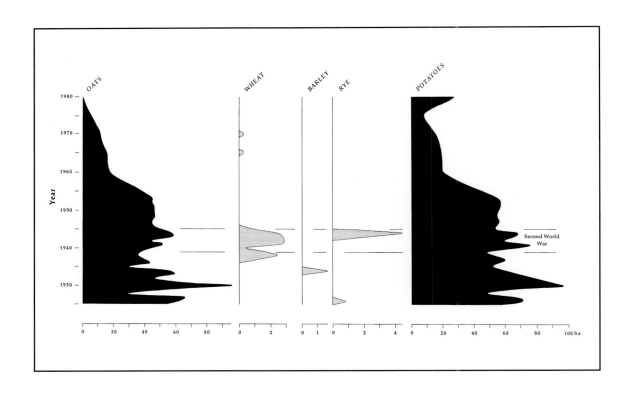

60

Fig. 9.3. Agricultural statistics showing the changing extent of arable farming in Renvyle during the period 1925-1980 (total area: 5500 hectares (13 600 acres)). The effects of the so-called compulsory tillage programme during the Second World War and the subsequent dramatic decline in arable farming and especially in cereals (almost exclusively oats) are notable features.

Fig. 9.4. An example of small scale tillage farming from Inishbofin that was typical of many parts of Connemara until the second half of this century. Oats, seen here with clearance heaps of stones, was the most common cereal, potatoes were also invariably sown (centre of photograph) as were root crops such as turnips (left hand side). The usual rotation consisted of oats, potatoes, root crop and oats followed by fallow. Cocks of hay have been taken in from the meadows and nearby is a clump of willow *(Salix)*, which was used as a source of scallops for thatching.

and there was increasing reliance on pastoral farming, and especially sheep farming with small scale arable farming continuing on a non-commercial basis (Fig. 9.4). Population levels, however, continued to decline. The 1950s and 1960s saw rural electrification, upgrading of the road network (the railway was closed in 1935) and the steady growth in tourism which by now had become an important part of the economy of the region. It also saw the beginnings of widescale afforestation by the state, the wisdom of which, from the commercial, environmental and tourist viewpoints, is open to question.

Ireland's entry to the European Economic Community (EEC) in 1973 has also had some profound implications for this remote region. In an effort to improve living conditions for its farmers, various farm support packages have been introduced. While the overall effects of these measures have been beneficial for the individual farmer, some have had undesirable side effects. The dramatic increase in sheep numbers during the last two decades, as a result of financial incentives, is a good example of an undesirable development from the environmental viewpoint. An unforeseen consequence of this has been severe overgrazing, especially of bogs and heathlands, which some believe may be the cause of the extensive peat erosion which is now taking place in many upland areas (Fig. 9.5).

In 1980, a National Park was established at Letterfrack which includes over 2000 ha of bog, heath and grassland. The establishment of a National Park marks an important and timely development, not least from the viewpoint of nature conservation. It ensures that at least a part of the Connemara landscape will be conserved for future generations to study, appreciate and enjoy.

Fig. 9.5. In the uplands of Connemara, the phenomenon of peat erosion is widespread. The photograph shows the erosion of peat, to bedrock in places, on the top of Binn Charrach, the Twelve Bens. While overgrazing by sheep certainly contributes to peat instability, it may not be the only factor involved.

Fig. 9.6. Despite appearances to the contrary, blanket bog resources are not inexhaustible. The photograph shows scraw being cut and saved as a source of fuel on Inishbofin where most of the blanket bog has long been cut away.

SUGGESTED FURTHER READING

EDWARDS, K.J. AND WARREN, W.P. (eds) 1985. *The Quaternary History of Ireland.* Academic Press, London.

FAIRLEY, J. 1984. *The Irish Beast Book* (2nd edn). Blackstaff Press, Belfast

GIBBONS, E. (ed.) 1991. *Hidden Connemara.* Connemara West Press.

Irish Countrywomen's Association 1985. *Portrait of a Parish. Ballynakill, Connemara.* Tully Cross I.C.A., Renvyle.

MITCHELL, F. 1986. *The Shell Guide to Reading the Irish Landscape.* Country House, Dublin.

MOLLOY, K. AND O'CONNELL, M. 1988. Neolithic agriculture — fresh evidence from Cleggan, Connemara. *Archaeology Ireland,* **2,** 67-70.

MOLLOY, K. AND O'CONNELL, M. 1993. Early land use and vegetation history at Derryinver Hill, Renvyle Peninsula, Co. Galway, Ireland. In: Chambers, F.M. (ed.), *Climatic Change and Human Impact on the Landscape*, pp. 185-199. Chapman and Hall, London.

MORRISSEY, J. AND FARRELL, B. 1987. *Inishbofin Connemara.* Crannóg Books, Dublin.

O'CONNELL, M. 1990. Origins of Irish lowland blanket bog. In: Doyle, G.J. (ed.), *Ecology and Conservation of Irish Peatlands,* pp. 49-71. Royal Irish Academy, Dublin.

O'CONNELL, M., MOLLOY, K. AND BOWLER, M. 1988. Post-glacial landscape evolution in Connemara, western Ireland with particular reference to woodland history. In: H.H. Birks, H.J.B. Birks, P.E. Kaland and D. Moe (eds), *The Cultural Landscape — Past, Present and Future,*pp. 487-514. Cambridge University Press, Cambridge.

ROBINSON, T. 1990. Connemara. Part 1: Introduction and Gazetteer; Part 2: a one-inch Map. Folding Landscapes, Roundstone.

WEBB, D.A. AND SCANNELL, M.J.P. 1983. Flora of Connemara and the Burren. Royal Dublin Society and Cambridge University Press.

WHILDE, T. 1994. *The Natural History of Connemara.* Immel Publishing, London.